Where Sunday Used to Be

Where Sunday Used to Be

New and Selected Poems

Daniel Klawitter

Foreword by David J. Rothman

RESOURCE *Publications* · Eugene, Oregon

WHERE SUNDAY USED TO BE
New and Selected Poems

Copyright © 2022 Daniel Klawitter. All rights reserved. Except for brief quotations in critical publications or reviews, no part of this book may be reproduced in any manner without prior written permission from the publisher. Write: Permissions, Wipf and Stock Publishers, 199 W. 8th Ave., Suite 3, Eugene, OR 97401.

Resource Publications
An Imprint of Wipf and Stock Publishers
199 W. 8th Ave., Suite 3
Eugene, OR 97401

www.wipfandstock.com

PAPERBACK ISBN: 978-1-6667-5951-8
HARDCOVER ISBN: 978-1-6667-5952-5
EBOOK ISBN: 978-1-6667-5953-2

10/04/22

All poems with Scripture quotations in this book are from the King James Version of the Bible (in the public domain) with the exception of Psalm 42:1, Proverbs 31:6, 2 Kings 2:23–24, and Ezekiel 23:20, which are from the New International Version®, NIV®. Copyright © 1973, 1978, 1984, 2011 by Biblica, Inc.™ Used by permission of Zondervan. All rights reserved worldwide. www.zondervan.com The "NIV" and "New International Version" are trademarks registered in the United States Patent and Trademark Office by Biblica, Inc.™

This book is dedicated to the memory of Theater Arts educator Jim Boman (b. July 18, 1940—d. March 24, 2021). A member of the Texas Thespian Hall of Fame, Jim spent 42 years teaching High School students in the Lone Star State (including this author) not just the magic of the dramatic arts, but the magic sparking inside all of us. As William Arthur Ward (another Texan) once put it: "The mediocre teacher tells. The good teacher explains. The superior teacher demonstrates. The great teacher inspires." Jim Boman was an inspiration to thousands.

Contents

Foreword by David J. Rothman | xi
Acknowledgements | xv

I. New Poems
The Pandemics of America, 2020 | 3
Afterlife with Borges | 5
Mixology | 7
A College Collage | 8
The Ballad of Miranda McAfee | 9
A Sinner's Song | 11
The Boys of Bethel | 14
Bless Your Heart Sonnet | 15
As You Like It (or Not) | 16
A Prophecy | 17
Take It All Off, Slowly | 18
Listening to Bulerias de la Nina Mora | 19
Preface to an Ontological Cookbook | 20
A Ghazal for Compassion Fatigue | 21

II. Poems from *A Poet Playing Doctor* (White Violet Press)
An Epistemology of Flesh | 25
Ihsan | 26
Evolution | 27
The Turning | 29
The Calm Before the Storm | 31
Her Mythological Temptation | 32
Writing a Poem Before My Wife Gets Out
  of Bed on the Weekend | 33
Catching Chickens | 34
Lunch at Corafaye's | 35

Fallen Angels | 37
What All Cats Know | 38
My Father's Offhand Reply | 39
Remembering Jason | 41
Pomegranates | 42
A Short Ode to Sausage | 43
Marxist Pillow Talk | 44
A Mystery | 45
Santa Fe, New Mexico | 46
Comrades | 47
Crossing the Border | 48
The Last Laugh of Tommy Lee | 50
Concluding Unscientific Postscript to Kierkegaard | 52
Repent! | 54
Why Go to Church? | 55
Zealots | 56
The Third Deadly Sin | 58
Land of Promise | 59
Runaway Muse | 60

III. Poems from *Put on Your Silly Pants* (Daffydowndilly Press) and *The Trickster: Poems for Very Clever Children and Silly Adults* (Whitebird Publications)
The Greatest Poet Who Has Ever Lived | 65
None Too Clever | 66
If I Were Edgar Allen Poe | 67
The Trickster | 68
Wild! | 69
I Want to Go to Narnia | 70
I Dreamed I Saw Shel Silverstein | 71
Haters | 72
A Story and a Lie | 73
The Book of St. Albans | 74

IV. Poems from *Plato Poetica* (White Violet Press)
Road Trip | 77
Speech Pathology | 79

Maybe God Is a Cat | 81
The Virtue of Brevity | 82
The Most Shameful Thing | 83
The Curse of the Uncaptivated | 85
Her Own Worst Enemy | 86
Magicians | 87
Scaremongering | 89
Haunted House | 90
He Contained Multitudes | 91
A Gouge in the Ground? | 92
C- | 93
Overflow and Commitment | 94
The Professor Who Could Hold His Liquor | 96
Departure | 97

V. Poems from *Quiet Insurrections* (Kelsay Books)
The Poem Behind the Poem | 101
In Defense of Intellectual Labor | 102
An Invitation | 103
Such Strange Pageantry | 104
A Flock Made Flesh | 105
Frogs in Texas | 106
Here There Be Monsters | 107
Goodness Gracious | 108
That Damn Goose | 109
Condensery | 110
Go Cat Go! | 112
Smartphone Revelations | 113
In Memory of Robert W. King | 114
Heavy Elements | 115
At the Franciscan Retreat Center, Colorado Springs | 116

VI. Poems from *The Misuse of Scripture*
(Independently Published)
Writing the Vision | 121
Bottoms Up | 122
Linguistics | 123

Grief Is . . . | 124
Yes, but Does He Write You Poetry? | 125
Cross-Stitch and Cross-Purposes | 126
Red Stuff | 128
For What It's Worth | 129
In Sickness and in Health | 130
Such Weariness | 131

About the Author | 133

Foreword

David J. Rothman

Daniel Klawitter's important new book presents fourteen fresh lyrics along with many others from his previous six collections. All of this work has a number of strengths, not the least of which is Klawitter's craft. His meters and rhymes are accomplished, fluid and playful. He also has a sense of humor at times whimsical and at others sharp, a forthright and compelling approach to his Christian faith, and learning both broad and deep that he wears gracefully. Most importantly, all these virtues appear under the aegis of a poetic quality rare in any time and almost dead in our own: wit.

Poetic wit is a serious matter. It is far more than humor or comedy. It is also notoriously difficult to define. In Cowley's "Ode of Wit," which Samuel Johnson described as "almost without a rival" more than a century later, the earlier poet begins by saying to an unnamed listener, presumably a gifted and witty poet, "Tell me, O tell, what kind of thing is wit, / Thou who master art of it." Cowley then says, no fewer than eight times, what wit is not. According to Cowley, wit is not a tale, or a jest, nor florid talk, or the forcing of verses without reason, or mere words that adorn or gild ideas, or language games (like acrostics), or a form of rage, and it must neither obtrude nor create merely the odd similitude. Finally he asks "What is it then, which like the power divine / We only can by negatives define?" Yet when he answers, he still evades:

> In a true piece of wit all things must be;
>   Yet all things there agree.
> As in the ark, join'd without force or strife,
> All creatures dwelt; all creatures that had life.

Foreword

Like many strong pieces of wit ancient and modern, Cowley's Ode answers with a riddle, telling us only that wit is comprehensive, harmonious, unified, and gives the feeling of life itself, a universal rhetoric that must include all things. Rather a tall order. And that is more or less where he leaves the matter, returning to his unnamed poet in his final couplet:

> Correct my error with thy pen;
> And if any ask me then,
> What thing right wit, and height of genius is,
> I'll only shew your lines, and say 'Tis this.

A cunning circle.

Though Johnson admires a great deal in Cowley, the poets he terms "Metaphysical" (preeminently Donne and Cowley, but also Cleveland and others) generally annoy him. Indeed, he spends pages in his life of Cowley harshly criticizing his work and calling passages "unnatural," "grossly absurd," "indelicate and disgusting" and concerned only with its own novelty and ambition.

T. S. Eliot's response to Johnson in his 1921 review of Grierson's anthology of metaphysical poets permanently renovated their reputations. Eliot directly counters Johnson's critique and argues that in the best Metaphysicals "there is a direct sensuous apprehension of thought or a recreation of thought into feeling." For Eliot, the Metaphysicals may be extravagant, but they do not yoke heterogeneous ideas together by violence, as Johnson argued; rather, at their best, they epitomize a unified poetic awareness in which cunning and craft create "a mechanism of sensibility which could devour any kind of experience," from the sensual to the intellectual. For Eliot, this is an apex of English poetry, after which began the "dissociation of sensibility" in which entire realms of experience became estranged from each other, as poets "thought and felt by fits, unbalanced." Eliot suggests that wit, if it may not contain all things, can at least consider them all.

This brings us to Klawitter, who is not an extravagant Metaphysical, but one of whose great strengths is the ability both to feel thoughts and to think with and through feeling. He is a poet who

Foreword

has not lost his wits, but rather cultivated them. This is evident from the opening of the very first poem in the book, "The Pandemics of America, 2020":

> There's a God-sized hole
> Where Sunday used to be
> And the ants are swarming
> The cast-off shell of a cicada.
>
> Bless the Lord, O my soul—
> And answer the croaking plea
> Of thy people in mourning
> As a falcon glides over the mesa.

Note the careful ghosting of meter and the subtle rhyming in corresponding lines from stanza to stanza. At the same time note the movement from spiritual agony to careful observation of the creation. Klawitter refrains from any easy equivalences between the two dimensions, which makes the connection only that much more powerful. The human, the divine, and the natural world coexist without discursive rationale. This is perhaps darkly humorous. The ants, cicada, falcon and mesa are indifferent to our suffering and alienation from God. At the same time, it suggests the sublime and poignant, as these phenomena are not only disjunct, but also, on second thought, continuous, if only we can see more deeply. That thought is felt, and the feeling is thought. And we must think feelingly and feel thoughtfully to connect them. Wit can run deep.

Wit is rare and always risky. The stakes are high and no one succeeds every time. Yet in his best passages and poems Klawitter rings its bell again and again. At times overtly humorous, at others deadly serious, at times intensely political, at others by turns learned and devout, he is always striving to be both thoughtful and sensual. Here is the full text of "A Prophecy":

> For now, the buzzards float
> Counterclockwise
> In a sky of exceptional blue.
> But the inevitable
> Shall come to pass:
> A carcass and a rendezvous.

Foreword

The first half is rich with detail: we see not only the buzzards, but the direction of their flight; not only the sky, but this specific sky. Then, in the second half comes the commentary, which is hardly a prophecy, but rather an acknowledgment of inevitable mortality. The specific feeling has become an idea. Finally, consider the etymology of "rendezvous," which in the French derives from an imperative in a military context, i.e. "present yourselves." We laugh at the irony, and then the trap snaps shut. Perhaps the speaker is observing a dying animal. But he hasn't named it, so the obvious suggests itself: perhaps he is that animal himself. And then we realize: so are we. Such is the reach of wit.

Every ambitious poet has flaws. Sometimes Klawitter's reach exceeds his grasp. It is unsurprising that a Master of Divinity might occasionally allow himself a sermon, and sermons are generally too pointed to be as suggestive as a poem like "A Prophecy." Yet that is rare, and there are dozens of poems in this book which are exemplary in marrying thought to feeling, an admirable goal for any poet, let alone a self-described Christianized Platonist. Particularly impressive are the poems in section IV, from Klawitter's book *Plato Poetica*, each of which begins with an epigraph from a wide range of Platonic sources. In one of those poems, "The Curse of the Uncaptivated," he writes "No virtue can redeem the loss of wonder," and this book bears out a sustained effort to give that ambition wings. But we should expect no less from a poet whose last name spells out, as its middle syllable, one of his greatest gifts.

Acknowledgements

The author thanks the editors of the following anthologies, journals, magazines, newspapers, and poetry websites for publishing most of the poems included in this collection, though often in previous versions:

Ancient Paths Literary Magazine, The Australia Times, The Beatnik Cowboy, Better Than Starbucks, Bristlecone, Carty's Poetry Journal, The Caterpillar, Colorado Life Magazine, Cyclamens & Swords, Dead Snakes, Episcopal Cafe, Fellowship & Fairydust, Front Porch Newspaper, The Galway Review, The Gateway Review, Journal of South Texas English Studies, Light, Lyrical Passion Poetry E-zine, Mad Swirl, Nomos Journal, The People's Tribune, Plough Quarterly, Poems and Poetry, The Poet Community, The Progressive Christian, Pulse: Voices from the Heart of Medicine, Rainy Day Poems, Sacramental Life, Shot Glass Journal, The Smoking Poet, Social Justice Poetry, Søren Kierkegaard Newsletter, Stinkwaves Magazine, Think Journal, Time of Singing: A Christian Literary Magazine, Trails of Hope and Terror, VerseWrights, The Voices Project, Wayfarer: A Journal of Contemplative Literature, Your Hands Your Mouth, Train River Publications, Uppagus, and *Vita Brevis.*

I.

New Poems

The Pandemics of America, 2020

I.

There's a God-sized hole
Where Sunday used to be
And the ants are swarming
The cast-off shell of a cicada.

Bless the Lord, O my soul—
And answer the croaking pleas
Of thy people in mourning
As a falcon glides over the mesa.

II.

You know, the White House seems
Aptly named and rather strident:
Occupied by a pale-faced tyrant—
A mumble-mouthed misogynist,

An Emperor of all ugliness
Who can only sneer and seethe.
There is a giant knee upon our necks:
A denial of the right to breathe.

III.

Those who go maskless
Still wear a mask

Of spiteful pox and pestilence.
You can whitewash
The white supremacy—
But you cannot hide
The malevolence.

And there's a God-sized hole
Where Sunday used to be.
The police are on patrol—
And Christ hangs on the tree.

Afterlife with Borges

*I have always imagined that Paradise
will be a kind of library.*

—BORGES

We were stalked relentlessly by tigers
Inside an adversarial athenaeum
Of horrific hieroglyphics
And mocking mirrors—
As books from other writers
Kept multiplying like our terror
On the expanding, capacious shelves.

Someone once said that if God is dead
Then everything is permitted.
But what could be more audacious
Than a labyrinth full of trilogies
With every third volume omitted?
This is not quite the paradise
We had hoped for or imagined.

And speaking on behalf of all
Our abandoned companions:
Are any of us truly transparent?
Even ghosts seem to wear
Such terribly haunted clothes.
Perfect clarity is as rare
As translucent roses:
There is just so much to *unsee*
In the afterlife's undaunted library.

We close our eyes and as Borges turns to go
A familiar song begins playing
On some ethereal piano
High up above in the firmament.
We try to sing along . . . but the words
Have lost all permanence.

Mixology

The earth is shaken and stirred.
The martini is one part vermouth.
Your vision is bloodied and blurred
And gone is the garnish of youth.

The martini is one part vermouth.
The olives are plucked from the tree.
And gone is the garnish of youth.
A devil is in the debris.

The olives are plucked from the tree.
There's no gin without the juniper.
A devil is in the debris.
So carry your cross like a crucifer.

There's no gin without the juniper.
No prayer that's gone unheard.
So carry your cross like a crucifer.
The earth is shaken and stirred.

A College Collage

I.

We know less than we think
about life and drink—
but four years is forever.
As we mature, we must endure
the debts that make us beggars.

II.

Disguising his stink with scent—
the lonely undergraduate
becomes the fragrant flagellant.

III.

Into the slack-jawed maw of the future
we go: not knowing from whence or whither.
Stitched together with various sutures,
we curse at the weather
from our precarious perches.

The Ballad of Miranda McAfee

Come gather 'round me people
And a story you shall hear—
About Miranda McAfee
And her love affair with beer.

O never did she marry,
She did not want a man.
She only wanted booze
In a bottle, glass, or can.

Her father was a bastard
And her brother a buffoon.
So Miranda spent her time
At the Lady Hearts Saloon.

She started her own brewery
And never had a doubt
That she could make a living
From pilsner, ale, and stout.

She became a famous woman
In the land of Honalee.
So raise your glass to the lovely lass
Miss Miranda McAfee!

Some men still tried to wed her,
But all of them did fail.
They just desired her fortune.
She told them to go to hell.

And the moral of this story,
I hope you understand—
Is you can brew a better beer
But not brew a better man.

A Sinner's Song

All the things I conquer
They come back like fate.
And the things I treasure
Become the things I hate.
I want a heart like Jesus
But I ain't no saint.
See my fallen halo?
I pick it up too late.

I wrestle with my demons
But I sometimes let them win.
And if you don't believe me
Just ask dear Rosalyn.
She will say I'm spineless
Though I'm a vertebrate.
See my fallen halo?
I pick it up too late.

I surely ain't no angel
I never claimed I was.
And sometimes if I'm drinking
I'm a little more than buzzed.
The preacher man on Sunday
Said: "God don't make mistakes."
See my fallen halo?
I pick it up too late.

I make my resolutions
But I know my will is weak.
I have the best intentions
But I *always* spring a leak.
I'm like a broken building,
You forgot to renovate.
See my fallen halo?
I pick it up too late.

I used to have more courage
I used to be admired.
I'm not sure how it happened
But my bravery expired.
If you gave me a kingdom
I'd surely abdicate.
See my fallen halo?
I pick it up too late.

We all have our temptations
And mine has long black hair.
I know that she's no good for me
I know I should beware.
Of course, I shouldn't meet her
No, I should not fornicate.
See my fallen halo?
I pick it up too late.

All the dice are loaded
And I won't play the game.
All the lies exploded
And now there's just the flame.
A candle in the darkness
Helps me to contemplate.
But see my fallen halo?
I pick it up too late.

Yes, all the things I conquer
They come back like fate.
I know I should resist this
But still I hesitate.
And in my weed-choked garden
No good seed will germinate.
See my fallen halo?
I picked it up too late.

The Boys of Bethel

> *From there Elisha went up to Bethel. As he was walking*
> *along the road, some boys came out of the town and jeered at him.*
> *"Get out of here, baldy!" they said. "Get out of here, baldy!"*
> *He turned around, looked at them and called down a curse on them*
> *in the name of the Lord. Then two bears came out of the woods*
> *and mauled forty-two of the boys.*
>
> —2 KINGS 2:23–24

The Boys of Bethel were not successful
In making the prophet smile.
They sought to tease but with expertise
He smote the juveniles!

The Boys of Bethel were simply bored
And looking for a distraction.
But fearful is the wrath of the Lord
When untempered by compassion.

The Boys of Bethel should have known
Elisha's humorless reputation.
Words alone can't break your bones,
But some words can lead to predation.

Bless Your Heart Sonnet

You been conceited since the day you was born.
Walking around with your nose so dang high
In the air, you could drown in a rainstorm!
You no apple pie on the fourth of July.
You no sweet tea on a warm summer day:
More like spoilt milk—in case you forgot it.
Strutting around in your new lingerie,
But no one gonna write *you* a sonnet.
I swear to Gawd woman, you smash me to bits
And our time together is cattywampus.
You can kiss my behind and kiss my grits.
You ain't no Georgia peach, you just pompous.
But bless your heart, you sure did butter my biscuit!
And when you sizzle like bacon? Cain't resist it.

As You Like It (or Not)

If you like, I can be your anti-sonnet:
That unappealing vomit in the corner
Causing you to retch in less than 14 lines
With a rhyme scheme that chimes off pattern.
Let me be your garish lantern of illumination
And you can be the subject of my non-flirtation.
It's better this way, to woo by not wooing.
My studied indifference is a way of pursuing
Your undivided and absolute attention.
It may be misguided; I make no apology.
This anti-sonnet is reverse psychology.

A Prophecy

For now, the buzzards float
Counterclockwise
In a sky of exceptional blue.
But the inevitable
Shall come to pass:
A carcass and a rendezvous.

Take It All Off, Slowly

Some leaves are the color of lust,
Or speckled gold and burnt sienna.
The spectacle of Fall is a carnival:
Bold flashes among the branches
In this sun-freckled fiesta of September.
The aspens turn and then they shimmer,
As the leaves peel off like garments—
Flung at the feet of a stripper.

Listening to Bulerias de la Nina Mora

The most important thing in flamenco is passion.
    —SARA BARAS

You could swear
The guitarist has birds for hands:
The flashing fingers take flight
Across the fretboard
Before her warbling wail
Breaks in—
A lamentation of need
As urgent as any animal's.
The guttural cry
Is spectacular
And then the rhythmic claps
As Rodrigo slaps the strings.
Once, you were dry as kindling—
You thought yourself inflammable.
But now your blood begins to sing
Stronger than caffeine
As you stifle a strangled shout—
Suddenly remembering
That the soul is a burning coal
No amount of heel stomps
Can stamp out.

Preface to an Ontological Cookbook

For me, the cooking life has been a long love affair,
with moments both sublime and ridiculous.
　　—ANTHONY BOURDAIN

It may be that hunger and love
Are twins from the same Mother—
An eternal longing to lull our lack.
And the presence of an absence
Is the recurring attack of history.
To ingest such fictions or facts
Is an ordeal beyond all endurance:
As you step back to your private pantry
Where no meal can bring assurance.

A Ghazal for Compassion Fatigue

Oh mama, the world is wet with weeping again.
Oh papa, the storm-tossed and lost are sleeping again.

When hope is double-crossed, the cost can be severe.
How often can hardened hearts start beating again?

The trauma that we all hear is a mantra of fear.
A litany of terrors and errors repeating again.

The stretcher-bearers bear the bodies from the rubble.
But why be too troubled with all that bleeding again?

We are punished and pummeled, worried and wearied.
But all things buried will soon start pleading again.

II.

Poems from *A Poet Playing Doctor*
(White Violet Press)

An Epistemology of Flesh

The suffering of the body
is most factual.
As real as a rock—
absolutely actual.

Pain is *certain* knowledge
on a cellular level:
an epistemology of flesh
as hard and sharp as metal.

But love can loom much larger
than what pain can comprehend.
So we turn to metaphysics
when we break instead of bend.

Ihsan

I would like to be impervious
and dangerous as a dervish
whirling with poems
bristling like swords
sharp enough to cut you.

And I would like to be spinning dizzy
with poetry sweet as opium,
eyes as sad as camels,
on a caravan towards utopia.

But most of all
I would like to be serene.
Not as a cloud
or corpulent bloodhound

but more like a Sufi
with poems purified clean,
inscrutable in their symmetry.

Evolution

When young,
you are tickled
with giggle sticks.
Poked and pinched
by playful primate fingers,
and lavished with kisses
from fur-covered lips.

Later—
bludgeoned half to death
by the monkeys
in the Public Zoo,
you are taunted
by brutish baboons
who despise you
because you're free.

And they simply
will not tolerate
a rebellious chimpanzee
who recites poetry.

Then—
tempted by a talisman
held in the hand of a man
in an impeccable suit,
you are shocked to discover
that he's just a gorilla
gorging himself on fruit.

The stench of his excrement
is overpowering
and you realize
that the time has come
for fight or flight.

To hell with Darwin, you decide . . .
this isn't about
the strongest surviving.
This is about the weak
standing upright.

The Turning

This is the time of our turning
like the red leaves you see
burning in November.

O god, my grief is a child
I hold as a thief
might hold his last night
of freedom . . .
desperate to my bones,
indelicate as tombstones
standing in the rain.

Sometimes pain is open like a prairie
(you can see it go on for miles),
or mysterious as a monastery
high atop snow mantled
mountain peaks.

As I study the zodiac,
who will speak to divine its meaning?
Distracted to death
by the sound of shadows
seething their prophecies
in the corner.

The scars you gave me
are still bleeding from the bondage
you keep me in,

reading your intentions
like a holy text.

O god, my grief—
Why do you squeeze my heart
until only the dregs are left
for drinking?

The Calm Before the Storm

It is just before
the other shoe drops.

The rabbit is feeding
and here comes the fox.

The seal in the ocean
is stalked by the shark.

The wolf among sheep
is all bite and no bark.

Her Mythological Temptation

She was both the seeker and the sought.
Caught between her village obligations
and the wilder places she had forgotten.

Married (unhappily) to a man made of metal,
his heart had long ago turned as pale
as a potato boiling in the kettle.

Now, many years later—
she hears the hooves
crunching the virgin snow.

She puts down her knitting,
looks out the window
and sees the satyr.

In the blue light of the moon
the frost on his flanks is as bright
as a polished mirror,

causing her majesty to swoon
high above the murky waters
of the moat.

The lady's dilemma is timeless:
Stay with the man of metal,
or run away with the half-man/half-goat?

Writing a Poem Before My Wife Gets Out of Bed on the Weekend

I have devoured the heart of the morning.
It was red and rich . . . a sun-drenched tomato.

Then I ate the crumbs of the hours before noon,
Softened with the milk of marvelous minutes

And crushed by the spoon of due diligence.

But all this time you have been sleeping!
The day has practically vanished.

Evening is for the insomniacs—
Sunrise is for the famished.

Catching Chickens

Morphine doesn't do much for dementia.
I know this because my grandmother
was trying to catch an imaginary chicken
on her deathbed.

Wanting to calm her fevered thrashing,
my sister cleverly said: "It's okay grandma.
I caught the chicken for you.
You can rest now."

But my grandmother's faded blue eyes
suddenly sprang wide open, and fixing my surprised
sister with a stern and lucid glare, declared:
"No, you did NOT!"

And I'm still uncertain which came first:
our nervous laughter or the shock of her clarity,
so unexpected, *we* almost died.

I guess we all have to catch our own chickens,
before we cross the road and reach that other side.

Lunch at Corafaye's

(A soul food restaurant)

The tongue is tied to recollection,
as thick as the good gravy
and as secretive as the collection
of recipes handed down like Scripture
from matriarch to daughter
in her family's ancestral tree.

Harken unto me when I tell you:
it's food that can make you cry.
This delicious genealogy
of fried okra; sweet potato pie.
Every taste is true from the black-eyed
peas to the candied yams,
the catfish and the "recession special"
Spam sandwiches.

It's just like I remember
in my grandmother's kitchen:
from the wood-paneled walls
to the sound of fried chicken
splattering in the pan.

If love can be measured
by food for the soul,
then we have been expanded
by a love so large

some may call it gluttony,
but I prefer *abundance*.
A feast with the fixings
free of charge.

Fallen Angels

There was something about the snow that day:
Flakes that fell like little angels to the ground—
Hands clasped in prayer, mouths soundless
As they spiraled down in star-bright sanctity
And melted away without a word or even a bell
In the church being rung. Nevertheless, I heard
A whispered *hallelujah*, as I caught one on my tongue.

What All Cats Know

Dogs are prose, and prone to please.
Mice are good for eating.
When moonlight splinters through the trees,
We watch humans while they're sleeping.
Disobedience is heroic.
It's wrong to persecute witches.
Hell is a world with no poets—
And heaven a charm of finches.

My Father's Offhand Reply

I wonder how many miles you walked
as a mailman
before your knees finally surrendered?

I wonder how many dogs you had to mace
in self-defense and
how many letters you faithfully delivered?

The distances you traveled
in Texas over the years
must truly be beyond all calculation.

I remember you coming home
soaked in sweat like salty tears
just wanting to unravel

but I would leap on your back
as if you were a horse
without a saddle

and greet you with my little boy's salutation:
"*Dada play toys! Dada play toys!*"

Recently reflecting on such childish joys,
I said to you:

"Man, that must have been a pain,
to come home after a long day of work
and have this little jerk

jumping all over you
demanding for you to play."

But your reply, dear father, stopped me short,
because I didn't expect you to suddenly say:
"Are you kidding me?
That was the *best* part of my whole damn day."

Remembering Jason

Picking pecans in the country for your father, their hard shells
were splintered beneath our nails. The crinkled nuts inside
were caramel-colored fortunes, rattling in our pails.
Growing restless, we made swords of fallen branches,
leaving your father to his harvest, while we stormed medieval
bastions and went roaming in the eye of the Beholder.

Shotguns rested on shoulders of adolescent bone
as we hunted squirrels, but found instead enchanted woods
of elves, gnomes, malicious trolls, and damsels in no distress.
Was anyone more distinctly and breathlessly blessed than us
in those ancient days of summer? With the world
a knowing whisper, and secrets shared like brothers?

Skinning a catfish fresh from the river, then a race on foot
to a magic tree that glimmered across a field of wilting beans.
At night, we spoke of God in the humid sky, old and bearded
and wise to our folly. I recall apple butter in the mornings
on toast, your father's cold-war ghosts that haunted his spleen.
Your mother softly singing: "Mr. Sandman, give me a dream."

A dream! Like a childhood redeemed in friendship.
Before our choices nudged us apart; before the questions got
harder, and our journeys took us farther than either of us had
bargained for. Some say that innocence can never be recovered.
But perhaps it is still there, somewhere in an orchard of pecans,
with the world a knowing whisper, just waiting to be discovered.

Pomegranates

My wife is on the couch,
peeling a pomegranate.
Ripping the rind and
plucking each red jewel
from the wreckage.

It is a bloody and laborious affair:
a ritual that I despair of
because I have no patience
for this Phoenician fruit.

When next I glance over,
she has the ruddy loot piled high
on a bone white napkin . . .

and the seeds look like tiny hearts,
offered in terrible tribute to a wife
who eats them like an Aztec goddess,
one by one, sacrifice after sacrifice.

A Short Ode to Sausage

Sad to say, there are people who regard lovers of sausages as relics from a kind of nutritional Dark Ages.
   —CHARLES SIMIC

Theologically, I'd say I was predestined
to eat animals carefully stuffed
inside their own intestines.

I'm the first to eat knockwurst,
and the last in a cholesterol tsunami
to relinquish my salami to the authorities.

Whether beef, lamb, or pork—
it will end up on my fork.
(I'm clear about my priorities.)

And for those who go into hysterics
proclaiming sausages barbaric,
I want you to understand:

That though you might be leaner
you can only have my wiener
if you pry it from my cold dead hands.

Marxist Pillow Talk

> In my opinion, true love is expressed in reserve, modesty, and even shyness toward his idol, and never in temperamental excesses or too premature intimacy.
>
> —KARL MARX, in a private letter, London, 1866

Come a little closer comrade
and I'll whisper my confession:

Nothing turns me on
like fighting against oppression!

In the midst of class struggle
there's *always* time to snuggle.

Who cares if we wake the neighbors
with the sounds of our surplus labors?

Seduce me my scarlet sweetie!
Let me give you a teasing tickle.

You got the hammer
and I've got the sickle.

Dialectical materialism
is the tune to which we dance.

Workers of the world unite!
There's an insurrection in our pants.

A Mystery

It's true that old age
has its own bouquet:
the remembered, fermented
wine of childhood
now uncorked,
left to breathe
in the dark cellar
of skin, bone, and memory.

For some, the past
is a mausoleum.
For others, a museum
full of curiosities.

Yet the greatest mystery
is not the history of Eden
but what lies ahead:

that second childhood
where we cross our hearts,
bow our heads
and hope to die
to rise again.

The last trumpet
and the last laugh is yours:
New wine will be poured
in new wineskins.

Santa Fe, New Mexico

I will meet you there beneath the turquoise sky
where honey is drizzled on a fresh sopapilla
and the days drip by so slow and gold and wise.

The sun so near it is God's own ancient eye
and the heavens are a warm, blue tortilla.
I will meet you there, beneath that turquoise sky.

Where the coyote sings his old, sly cry
while the Indians on the Plaza (*Viva La Raza!*)
walk by so slow and gold and wise.

At sunset the horizon spreads her purple thighs:
the air scented with pinyon and juniper.
We breathe it out in sighs, beneath a turquoise sky.

Here in the high desert where the air is oven-dry,
beauty becomes my artful executioner
and I die (like O'Keeffe): slow, gold, and wise.

But each morning after sleep brings yet another surprise.
Enchanted once again as your troubadour
when we greet each other beneath that bold, turquoise sky
and I meet you with holy faith: in days slow, gold, and wise.

Comrades

For all the dreams of dark-skinned men,
women and children,
scorched and stumbling on blistered feet.
For the nameless and numbered,
who were butchered like meat
with the sky growling thunder
and whose napalmed screams were silenced.

I offer you this hymn.

For the guns of defiance
and lips that curse . . .
for the peasants who barefoot
walk proud on the earth.
Hacked by machetes
and consumed in fire
or hung from trees
like electric wires of resistance!

I offer you this humble hymn.

Though death be persistent,
one truth stays consistent
in this song of our lament:
we may be cut down,
but we will always return,
like weeds through the cement.

Crossing the Border

It is a crime to be criminalized
for crossing a border
that crossed you first.

When will they realize
that walls made of mortar
can't contain the desperate thirst

for a better life
and a heavier purse
in the land of milk and honey?

It is a crime to be cursed
for speaking a language
that doesn't fit their Story.

And as for those who worship
the red, white, and blue
of Old Glory . . .

Well, let's just say it's usually true
that the people waving that flag
at you are neither red nor blue—

which leaves only one hue
that is, in fact, an accident
of pigmentation.

That no human being is illegal
in the eyes of the angels
seems to escape their imagination.

And as the cries of "Go back to Mexico!"
arise with righteous indignation,
I wonder what these patriots will do

when they finally march on through
the door of death and come at last to
the guarded gate of God's own town . . .

And discover to their horror,
that Jesus crossed the border
and Jesus Christ is *brown*.

The Last Laugh of Tommy Lee

> *The cock doth craw, the day doth daw*
> *The channerin' worm doth chide:*
> *Gin we be mist out o' our place,*
> *A sair pain we maun bide.*
>
> —*THE WIFE OF USHER'S WELL*, traditional folk ballad

Some people just can't take a joke.
But Tommy Lee found funny
almost everywhere he looked.

Had he been a stand-up comic
he may have made good money,
or as an author of children's books.

But Tommy Lee worked in the factory.
And like a kid who never grows up
he was an obsessive practical joker.

Looking back, it's a miracle
he was never fired, but people say he was
universally admired by his co-workers.

Then one afternoon, Tommy's fingers
got caught in the machine. And it cut him
clean to both wrists, leaving only stumps.

For two whole days, Tommy's tongue

was quiet. Then he awoke to the smell
of the hospital, recalled the industrial violence,

and he began to understand:
(he would never work again.)
On the third day, his mother came in,

and she saw Tommy's chest expand.
And while she cried, Tommy Lee died,
saying: "Look ma, no hands."

Concluding Unscientific Postscript to Kierkegaard

> *People understand me so little that they do not even understand when I complain of being misunderstood.*
>
> —SØREN KIERKEGAARD, *Journals*, Feb. 1836

Though your books line my shelf
dog-eared and underlined,
I can't claim to fully understand *myself*—
much less a mind as refined as yours.

You were one smart egg—
though legend has it
a hunchback with weak legs
and a handsome face.

A gloomy Dane who traced
relentlessly, the hypocrisies
of the bourgeoisie—
the semiotics of invisibility.

Preoccupied with paradox and sin,
you wrote under several false names,
then later played the game
of attacking your own pseudonyms.

And I love how you walked
the crooked streets of Copenhagen,

where often you would pause and talk
with the poor, the hungry, the forsaken.

You were no philosopher secluded
in an ivory tower, deluded
with visions of power and
fake heroics—Søren: you were no Stoic.

In fact, there are over ninety references
in your corpus where you call yourself a poet.
And *that* is why you are misunderstood!
Because poets are as slippery as porpoises
skimming the surface, then diving to the depths.

We hold our breath and try to follow—
but this fear and trembling,
is a sickness unto death—
an existential wallow.

And though your books line my shelf—
their spines cracked and pages brittle,
I may not understand myself—
and understood you little.

Repent!

His spirit says no,
but his flesh says yes.
He is a man compressed
into the smallest of spaces.

An evangelist
of the black and white
blood at midnight
apocalypse.

It is hard to ignore
the spittle of judgment
that spews from his lips.
But what he hates most
is that which resists
his will—himself!

He is the maker of his own cages.
See how red his face is?

God, I hope the end
of the world is nigh
for these miniscule men
and their unconscious
self-hatreds.

Why Go to Church?

Because I'm a hypocrite
and so are you.
And it is good gospel

to have this truth
revealed, rehearsed,
and reviewed

in a community of
the wounded and
the anointed.

If you are looking for
perfection, then you will
no doubt be disappointed.

For the church is filled
with sinners: with preachers,
popes, and pimps.

Of course religion is a crutch,
but what makes you think
you don't limp?

Zealots

(Or: My Argument with TV Evangelists)

The certainty
of a fanatic
makes me smile
to mask my panic.

The truth is:

I pity them
their lack of doubt—
their fascination
with damnation.

They want to shout you
into heaven
which is the worst kind
of salvation!

The moral
of the story
is this:

Moses encountered glory
in the burning
of the bush—

but sometimes God
is in a kiss—
in the *pull*-
and not the push.

The Third Deadly Sin

Whenever you feel that old familiar tug—
the babbling of the blood from a carnal stare,
or an over-friendly hug—

blame it on the wine you had with dinner.

And remember the prayer of St. Augustine
ye sensual sinners.
Take comfort and do not fret.
For even the Bishop of Hippo once said:

"Lord make me chaste. But not yet! Not yet!"

Land of Promise

(With a nod to Rabbi Hillel, 70 B.C.E.-10 C.E.)

I have seen your sacred hills
scarred by violence, but still holy—
in the way silence can be shrill
after breathing slowly

I have learned to stand as still
as the water in Jacob's Well.
Immobile as Lot's wife—
a soul of salt thirsty for redemption.

My gentile lips speak
with growing apprehension
about the ungentle.

Let speaking cease among the weary!

If it is for shalom, salaam, and peace
that we labor, then that which is hateful
do not do unto your neighbor . . .
everything else is commentary.

Runaway Muse

I will try to write today
though nothing may come.
The words with which
I've struggled
are too hard-won—
stubborn as mules
with drool dripping
off the tongue.

I've barely even begun,
but already
I'm sick to my stomach,
gagging on bitter grass.
These words are so unsteady,
they explode—
sear my soul to silence
and coat my throat like ash.

And though the pencil
is now a shovel
in my curious hand—
(scratching at the paper
like a frantic, furious madman
farming in the sand
for inspiration)—
it's still no use,
for all my fields lie fallow.

This is the best that I can offer
to my muse upon her altar . . .
so light a candle,
say a prayer—

and try again tomorrow.

III.

Poems from *Put on Your Silly Pants* and *The Trickster: Poems for Very Clever Children and Silly Adults*
(Daffydowndilly Press) and (Whitebird Publications)

The Greatest Poet Who Has Ever Lived

I'm the greatest poet who's ever lived.
Or at least the greatest who's just like me!
My awesome rhymes will blow your mind
Like a cinnamon-flavored breeze.

Yes my poems are so delicious
You eat them up like toast.
I'm sure you like other poets,
But like *my* poems the most.

My verses are entertaining.
And I'm sure that you'll agree:
My poems need no explaining,
You understand them perfectly.

Other poets are confusing
And they write to be obscure.
But me, I'm always amusing.
I'm not the sickness, I'm the cure.

None Too Clever

As long as you can remember,
People have always said:
"You are not the sharpest tool
In the history of tool sheds."

You are not the keenest knife
In your parent's kitchen drawer.
In your case the elevator
Doesn't reach the highest floor.

Some marbles may be missing;
Some little screws are loose.
The train has left the station.
And you are the caboose.

If I Were Edgar Allen Poe

If I were Edgar Allen Poe—
There're many things I'm sure I'd know:
Suspense, allure, and atmosphere—
Foreboding castles, full of fear.

I'd write of chatty and raving ravens—
Cats in walls and gloomy maidens.
Buried hearts that tick like clocks—
And bells that ring and never stop.

I'd invent the style: detective fiction;
And flaunt a gothic predilection.
I'd have a mustache, jet-black hair—
My eyes would have a haunted stare.

My fondness for intoxication—
Would bring on moods with strange vibrations:
Like a dark and raging sea,
Or chill, that took my Annabel Lee.

And folks would read my work today—
Despite its singsong, rhythmic sway.
These are a few things that I would know—
If I were Edgar Allen Poe.

The Trickster

Coyote creeps through raindrops
And slinks between the trees:
So crafty and so cunning
With a trick up every sleeve.

He likes the taste of porcupine
And has a sense of humor.
He gifted fire to humankind,
According to one rumor.

He's neither wolf nor dog,
But something in between.
Perhaps, he is a demigod
Who isn't what he seems.

Wild!

I like to feel the sunshine
And the grass beneath my feet.
I like to see the wily weeds
Peek up through hard concrete.

Some things we just cannot contain:
The wind, the truth, the sky—
Animals we can barely tame,
No matter how we try.

The world's an endless mystery
By which I am beguiled.
So I sing of liberation—
I sing of all things wild!

I Want to Go to Narnia

I want to go to Narnia
Where the animals can speak.
I want to meet King Aslan
And the mouse named Reepicheep.

I want to ride a centaur,
Which truly would be wondrous!
I want to cheer up Puddleglum
And have tea with Mr. Tumnus.

I want to go to Narnia
Where the River Shribble flows.
But the wardrobe in my house
Is only filled with clothes.

I Dreamed I Saw Shel Silverstein

I dreamed I saw Shel Silverstein
Alive as you or me.
His head was bare of any hair
As he hugged The Giving Tree.

I begged him for a song or two—
He picked up his guitar!
And sang about "A Boy Named Sue,"
Whose father had a scar.

And then we had a "Hug O' War"
Like the very best of friends.
I dreamed I saw Shel Silverstein
Down Where the Sidewalk Ends.

Haters

Some folks are good at hating.
It's all they've ever known.
They learned it from their parents
And practiced it at home.

I'm not sure why they do it,
But those who feel compelled
To hate those who are different
May really hate themselves.

A Story and a Lie

There is a crucial difference
Between a story and a lie.
A fable may be fiction,
But with a greater truth inside.

But a lie is a deception
For the liar's *own* protection,
And it spreads like an infection
If left without correction!

So, feel free to tell a story
To Jack and Jill and Sid.
But don't forget the difference
Between a story and a fib.

The Book of St. Albans

A murder of crows—
A gaggle of geese.
In poetry and prose—
An ancient masterpiece.
A parliament of owls
Or perhaps a scream of swifts?
You can feel it in your bowels:
Such luscious artifice!

IV.

Poems from *Plato Poetica*
(White Violet Press)

Road Trip

We should live out our lives playing at certain pastimes.
   —PLATO'S *Laws*

Cold Colorado morning.
The coffee percolates.
Elk are on the move in Evergreen.
They bellow their morning prayers
with breath like frosty incense
while drivers in their cars stare
and gesticulate in their direction.

We are all part of a herd.

We huddle together for warmth and protection.
Down in Denver the traffic is already terrific.
And I'm in the backyard, writing this poem—
thinking about Jack Kerouac
and getting that specific itch.
Wanting to get out on the road—
just drive and throw my cell phone
out the window into a ditch.

It's a tempting thought, I'll give you that:

To keep on driving
like Neal and Jack.
Drive until the tank is empty

and my belly full of breakfast:
Eggs over easy, bacon crisp and salty.
A road trip to a state of grace.
Becoming a different person—
just by going to a different place.

Speech Pathology

> *The most important thing to say
> hasn't been said yet.*
>
> —PLATO, *The Republic*, II

They whisper in your ear
But stop just short of what
You hope to hear
And can't articulate.

Your mouth is mush—
The unsaid phrase
You anticipate
Becomes: "*Hush* child, *hush*."

Why so hard to speak
When the garden of words
Is so lush? Why do your eyes
Leak and your cheeks blush?

That fearful fluency
That others trust
In us is non-transparency,
A dam that won't bust.

But even those who speak
Extemporaneously on their feet
With such seeming ease

And compelling candor—

Cannot exhaust or appease
The desire for language
To be *more* than precise.
It wants instead to meander

Beyond the limits of grammar
To the unthought-of thought
That causes one to stammer
In the fraught-filled speaking.

The best has not yet been said;
How hopeful to have overheard—
And silence is no cause for dread,
For it precedes the spoken Word.

Maybe God Is a Cat

> *It's something else you see in dogs,*
> *and it makes you wonder at the animal.*
>   —PLATO, Republic II

> *In 1911, the little town of Nakhla in Egypt was the scene of one of*
> *the most remarkable events in history: a chunk of rock*
> (later discovered to be a piece of the planet Mars)
> *fell from the sky and killed a dog, the only known canine fatality*
> *caused by a cosmic object.*
>   —PAUL DAVIES, *The Fifth Miracle*

Maybe God *is* a Cat—
Sharpening her claws on planets,
Pouncing from star to star
Unraveling our lives like yarn.

We scatter as mice in the barn,
Our hearts pitter-patter—
But there is nowhere to hide
If God is a celestial cat like that:

A feline God of War
Brighter than Blake's Tyger
Who knows what fangs are for
And never leaves survivors.

The Virtue of Brevity

> Socrates: *By Hera, Gorgias, I do like your answers.*
> *They couldn't be shorter!*
> Gorgias: *Yes, Socrates, I daresay*
> *I'm doing it quite nicely.*
>
>   —PLATO, *Gorgias*

O those long-winded preachers
I grew up listening to in the south!

On and on they'd beseech us—
With diarrhea of the mouth.

If you can't say it in 15 minutes,
Then I have but one retort:

No sinner has walked out on a sermon
Because it was too short.

The Most Shameful Thing

> *And now we've agreed that injustice, and corruption of soul as a whole, is the most shameful thing.*
>
> —PLATO, *Gorgias*

Forgive me father,
for I have lived
with good intentions.

But we all know
what the road
to hell is paved with.

Brick by brick
I've built my house
of horrors.

Slowly, over time
my deposits
gather relevance

and my closets
contain a graveyard
of skeletons.

Who am I,
an Augustus of injustice
to ask for absolution?

My sackcloth soul
is a waste of windswept ashes—
a hermitage of pollution.

As undisputed king
of the most
shameful thing,

the distance
between my words and actions
grew gradually.

An accumulation
of small hypocrisies
like a Greek tragedy

everyone else
can see coming
except the hero himself.

The Curse of the Uncaptivated

> *The unexamined life is not worth living.*
> —PLATO, *Apology*

A lack of curiosity
regarding the world outside your walls
(or worse—the world within you)
is a great sin. It is unforgivable.
No virtue can redeem the loss of wonder.
Unexamined certainties not pondered
lead only to unbelievable rigor mortis:
the mind turns turtle; the heart an armored tortoise.

If you find yourself captive in a room
where all the uncaptivated agree
there is nothing left to learn—
get out as soon as you can!
To wage war against all doubt
is an act of murder—understand?
It's as bad as killing a child
with your bare and blind-boned hands.

Her Own Worst Enemy

> *Be kind, for everyone you meet*
> *is fighting a hard battle.*
>
> —Falsely attributed to PLATO

Ah, now I see
how the best and the worst
fills the same mortal cup.

No use crying over
spilled blessings
or the curse of vicious circles.

The geometry of my
many-chambered heart
contains the strangest angles.

My best intentions
are a tangle of angels—
fallen and exalted.

Halt! Who goes there?
Oh, it's just me.
My doppelganger of stealth—

climbing the stairs
to declare: the stranger
danger of myself.

Magicians

> *Everything that deceives*
> *may be said to enchant.*
>
>   —PLATO, *Republic III*

Who doesn't love
a white rabbit
pulled from a black
top hat?

Or the restoration
of the woman who
underwent a smiling
dismemberment?

We all clap
for a good resurrection.
(Sleight of hand and
misdirection).

How did he *do* that?

An endless river
of scarves,
a vanishing coin;
levitating cards.

Chinese linking rings,
deadly swords and sabers.
Near death escapes
from sealed
water chambers.

Catch a bullet in the mouth?
No problem!
Get guillotined on stage?
He reappears unharmed

and your children
think it's awesome.

Of course we know
it's all an illusion—
and wishes are seldom
granted.

But a part of us
needs to believe:
in a domain beyond
deception—
a world re-enchanted.

Scaremongering

*When the tyrant has disposed of foreign enemies
by conquest or treaty, and there is nothing to fear from them,
then he is always stirring up some war or other, in order that
the people may require a leader.*

—PLATO, *Republic VIII*

Fear of the Other—Feeding the dragons
Herding the Sheep—Circle the wagons.
Make up the facts—(Facts don't matter.)
Battle is better—Unravel the banner.
War is a business—Fear is a fever.
You look suspicious—Follow the leader.

Haunted House

> *The house that has a library in it has a soul.*
> —Falsely attributed to PLATO

My house is *full* of spirits, haunting specters
Bound in books, each with their own
Unique appearance, smells, and textures.

So many souls speaking on the shelves
Texts in translation—ephemeral selves
In stories, plays, poems, and essays.

A home filled with such ambitions—
Is like phantom psychokinesis.
These literary apparitions permit us
To intone: *Abitus sed non oblitus.*

He Contained Multitudes

> *Then aren't there these two forms,*
> *largeness and smallness?*
>
> —PLATO, *Parmenides*

Walt Whitman's ambitions
were so large and ferocious
they filled an entire Kosmos!
Mine is a smaller gnosis—
a microscopic intuition,
a ghost almost imperceptible.
A poem that goes bump in the night.
My tiny poltergeist
of the philanthropic transaction:
Just watch me disappear
out of sight with satisfaction.
I am infinitesimal.
I contain so many subtractions.

A Gouge in the Ground?

> *For this is an experience which is characteristic of a philosopher, this wondering: this is where philosophy begins and nowhere else.*
>
> —PLATO, *Theaetetus*

You can say it is a gouge in the ground—
these gulches, gorges, arroyos, and canyons.
Shaped by water and time's ability to astound—
we walk with wonder as our constant companion.

Rivers run like arteries through some.
Others are dry as deserted desert sky.

But they all remind me of sculpture—
sheer art beneath the skin of seeming.
Above a gyration of circling vultures.
Below a cathedral beyond all believing.

C-

And whenever we disagree about number,
about many and few, who are the ones
who decide? Aren't they the ones who count?

　　—PLATO, *On Justice*

I was always below average at math.
Yet I know how fullness retracts
And shrinks back to empty.

How the calculus of loss
Is unequal to achievement,
Or simply: how all our numbers

In unencumbered joyful sequence—
Become balanced by our teachers
In the algebra of bereavement.

Overflow and Commitment

> *There is an old proverb, legislator, which we poets never tire of telling and which all laymen confirm, to the effect that when a poet takes his seat at the tripod of the Muse, he cannot control his thoughts. He's like a fountain where the water is allowed to gush forth unchecked.*
>
> —PLATO, *Laws IV*

The truth is the muse is often fickle.
She likes to be wooed.
Sometimes she wants to be tickled,
On other days, she is rude just to
Start a quarrel that ends in a kiss.

You scribble a line, but she
Wants to hear it oral, recited with
A twist of the tongue. Or she may
Want it sung with full lungs, before
She will bestow a laurel for your crown.

If you try to force it, you will only
Make her frown and bring yourself
A world of woe. Courting her
Requires daily discipline, attention
To form, detail, and apprehensions.

The slow hard work accumulates
Into the occasional grace of inspiration:
The poem that seems to spring from

Nowhere, fully formed and articulate,
An omnipotent storm of exaltation.

And *then* it flows like a fountain—
And you are drowned in words
You composed but don't know how
You did it. But the muse knows
Where water goes—it's all about
Commitment.

The Professor Who Could Hold His Liquor

*The lover of inquiry must follow his beloved
wherever it may lead him.*

—PLATO, *Euthyphro*

I am the scholar of your lips—
A not-neutral academic

Of the careful cartography of your hips—
Which demands an engaged partnership.

Your body is my dissertation—
The sole subject of my study.

And in my imagination—
You're like bourbon from Kentucky.

Well-aged and enjoyed in moderation.
Too much consumption offends proper modesty.

I take you instead in sips—
I drink you up responsibly.

Departure

> *The hour of departure has arrived, and we go our ways—*
> *I to die, and you to live. Which is better God only knows.*
>
> —PLATO, *Apology*

It is the way of all flesh and rust
That most things must come to an end.
What begins must stop, what was
Becomes what is not.

But some things remain. Not just
The DNA passed on to your descendants.
There are other remnants beyond
The grave and mortal coil of weakness.

To speak of it would spoil the secret.

This then is the end of a poem
That knows well what it can't disclose
While hoping for a sequel.
So for now, this poet of the people
Says goodbye, the end—Finito.

V.

Poems from *Quiet Insurrections*
(Kelsay Books)

The Poem Behind the Poem

I live in between the black ink
and white spaces of the page.
Your fingers graze the surface—
and I tremble. I can be as pliable
as a pillow, or stiff as steel.
Everything you feel I feel.
In the absence and lack I lurk—
the poem *behind* the poem.
And I am willing to work
on our relationship. I am a mind
waiting to meet you. I am nothing
without your gaze. Can you see me?
Not yet? No worries. I am patient.
Read on and be amazed.

In Defense of Intellectual Labor

It begins innocently enough
With a wondering.
With a however hung
On a what if.

With a maybe
Married to a possibility
Not yet exposed
Or explored.

Sure, there are answers—
Some of them are even
Convincing.

What is deplorable
Is thinking the obvious
Is obvious
Just for existing.

It requires
Some agility—
Some frisky flexibility
To not become distressed

When provoked
By a question
That turns into a quest.

An Invitation

*Yes, as everyone knows, meditation
and water are wedded forever.*

—HERMAN MELVILLE

Come, you soft-shelled poets filled with seawater.
Come and leak your speech on thirsty beaches!
Come and sing the ocean's primal power.
Come and christen the living dictionary.
Come and listen to the seas, the rivers, the lakes.
Come and offer tribute to the tributary.
Come and accompany the lute and the lyre.
Come and salute the shifting personas.
Come with your fuel for the original fire.
Come add your spice to the cauldron's aroma.
Yes, come and find your calling, your true vocation:
The marriage of mind to cherished hydration.

Such Strange Pageantry

*Remembrance of things past
is not necessarily the remembrance of things
as they were.*

—MARCEL PROUST

It is a strange alchemy—
To make the past present
Through an act of will
And remembrance.
To make it real
Though intangible,
While never leaving
The mind's labyrinths.

Such strange pageantry—
At times unpleasant
With regretful lament.
Time travel as penance
Is impractical—but still
We honor the Sabbath.
We keep it holy and we will
Unpack our baggage.

A Flock Made Flesh

The sudden birds erupt upwards
In a shower of stunning confetti—
Startled starlings taking wing.

Like my love in feathers
For you my dear darling—
When you turn and preen
So spectacularly.

Frogs in Texas

After the rainstorm—
a symphony of frogs!
A plague-like multitude,
a croaking catalog
of amorous amphibians,
hop-plopping in the grass
after a good soaking.
So glossy wet with gratitude—
they are green and obscene
and glamorous.
Somewhere there is a
great god of frogs
who conducts this cacophony
of guttural, semi-permeable
pornography.

Here There Be Monsters

One cannot slay an absent dragon.
—PERCIVAL EVERETT

And so, I slew myself. Not a suicide, but a surgery—
A crusade against the ravenous dragon of the heart.
Green and serpentine as envy; slithering like greed.
The serpent hoards the hurts it needs.
Coiled and constricting around the glistening rot
As the forked tongue flickers, hissing its forget-me-nots.
    The harrowing of hell begins at home.
    Alone with our home-grown hazards:
The hand upon the hilt—the sword oiled within the scabbard.

Goodness Gracious

Silence made everything resonate.
—GEORGE PROCHNIK

It is so quiet
The landscape itself
Seems pious:
The hallowed hills,
The prostrate fields—
Even the flowers
Bow their ostentatious
Heads in silent prayer.
And in all this humble
Goodness graciousness
I find myself there:
A clumsy, cursing
Stranger—nature
Looking at nature.
And what is worse:
The quiet seems
Unnatural—
My place in it
Perverse.

That Damn Goose

> *This should not be taken lightly, we have had reports of broken noses, broken ribs and even deaths caused by Canada geese attacks.*
>   —OHIO GEESE CONTROL WEBSITE

I swear that damn goose with the glassy eyes is out to get me.
So much foul madness in such a ferocious fowl.
Every time I walk by, he starts to high step like a Nazi.
I watch him warily from the safety of the balcony,
As Wagner's *Flight of the Valkyries* plays in the background.

That damn goose is as strong as Zeus, with his thunderbolt beak
And his hissing mouth of Hades. Can geese have rabies?
I swear he is half-cobra with his arching neck and venomous face:
The rough and brutal beast foretold by William Butler Yeats—
The most vicious Canadian goose in the entire United States!

Condensery

It is a made-up word.
It means: 13 ways
Of baking a blackbird
In a pie. Layers upon layers.
And beneath the crust
A festival of flavors:
Earth, worm, seed, sky.

The density of it
Does you a favor:
You taste compression—
And concentration.
Distilled like whiskey—
Now condensation
Gathers on the glass
You vaguely resemble.

A poem hugged snug
Is a pig in a blanket!
A single poem can wear
So many clothes
Other poems are naked.

Not all are
Equally skilled
At seduction.
Some poems wink—

Others reek
With the pungent
Perfume of skunk.

And sometimes,
It just implodes
Under the weight
Of sound and sense.
The poem with
Cake-like ambitions
Collapses and shrinks—
Condensed.

Go Cat Go!

> *If it weren't for the rocks in its bed,*
> *the stream would have no song.*
>
> —CARL PERKINS

If it weren't for Carl Perkins—
That fingerpicking star
Of ardent arpeggios
On his Gibson guitar—
We wouldn't have
That contagious
Cool cat serenade
About those famous
Blue suede shoes
That rocked the country
Senseless
From the humid heat
Of his home in Memphis, TN.

The toe-tapping
Son of sharecroppers
Forsook the fields
And became the Dixie fried,
Awesome apostle
Of rockabilly's gospel.
Can I get an amen?
Glory Hallelujah!
Listen up all mama's children:
Just a Little Dab'll Do Ya.

Smartphone Revelations

> *I feel about my phone the way horror-movie*
> *ventriloquists feel about their dummies: It's smarter*
> *than me, better than me, and I will kill anyone*
> *who comes between us.*
>
> —COLSON WHITEHEAD

I am a jealous god and very zealous for your adoration:
Your face consecrated in the blaze of my holy light—
Your gaze held fast as any enchanted Narcissus.
I fit in your hand, but I am the sacred object
Of your daily rituals. It is *you* who obeys
All my commands to the letter—even when
My directions are suggestive or capricious.
Worship me when you're crossing the street on foot!—
Oblivious to oncoming traffic . . . head bowed in prayer
Like an unaware monastic. Your eyes so rapt
With faithful veneration. *You shall have no gods*
Before me—is the law of my congregation.

In Memory of Robert W. King

1937–2017

(Bob King was the founder of the Colorado Poet's Center
and the author of the full-length poetry collections
Old Man Laughing and *Some of These Days*.)

Some of These Days go by too fast,
But deep down we all know
The days don't last regardless.
We all miss his voice of course:
The sound of honest sandpaper
Or gravel gurgling
In a rough, riverbed.
He could hold you, spellbound,
At a poetry reading,
Becoming everyone's
Favorite grandpa in verse.
Thank the muses we still have his work:
Poems which slide on the mind
Like well-washed jeans,
Loose and tight in all the right places—
Good for pacing the distances
Between hope and hopelessness.
From now on when the sages ask:
"What is the sound of one hand clapping?"
I will always think of you, Bob,
And the sound of an *Old Man Laughing*.

Heavy Elements

The lightning rips
A seam of sky
Wide open:
Slashing a gash
Through night's
Ink-splashed manuscript.

And the stars are
The trillion eyes
Of an unseen god—
Each eye lit
Like a candle wick
To illuminate or ignite

Our parchment
Papered hearts:
Our weeping wax
And sticky pitch—
All our combustible
Bits and parts

That come from
The same stuff of stars—
(So we've been told).
Formed in the furnace
Of a cosmic bonfire:
Unimaginably old.

At the Franciscan Retreat Center, Colorado Springs

*As the deer pants for streams of water,
so my soul pants for you, my God.*

—PSALM 42:1

A congregation of devout deer
appeared over the hill
and came down to graze
on a Eucharist of leaves:

The new, green goodness
of God's good spring.

Initially, there was no rapture
just a rupture in my reverie.

I had no idea what might occur:
smoking my cigarette outside
like a thurifer.

It didn't seem to bother them though,
the smoke. They must have known
I wasn't a wildfire.
Just another man sacrificing himself
in the wilderness.

And then, with magnificent tenderness,
one of the deer got so near to me . . .
20 feet or less. We were now
in the same sanctuary of grass.

For some reason I looked away and
stretched out my left hand
thinking: "This too shall pass."
But it did not.

The deer approached without fear
his black nose nuzzled
my palm, the nostrils flaring.
And that was it.
Who blessed who I don't know.
But he left as gentle
as a penitent.

VI.

Poems from *The Misuse of Scripture*
(Independently Published)

Writing the Vision

*And the Lord answered me, and said, 'Write the vision,
and make it plain upon tablets, that he may run that readeth it.'*

—HABAKKUK 2:2

Here in the rot and wreck—
In the besotted and messy elegance
Of my chosen art, I strive and crawl
Through broken psalms
Of complaint and praise toward
What? Irrelevance? Only time will tell
If desire is equal to intelligence.
And even if it isn't, at least I have dwelled
In the temple of the most highs.
I have seen them ascend
Like Perseus on Pegasus:
These poets with their mysteries—
Their uncanny focus and eloquence.
They help us to see beyond the charms
Of sight. And by their liturgies
They sing us home to where we
Are infused with such reflected light
The darkness is quite undone:
Stunned, illuminated, and incredulous.

Bottoms Up

> *Let beer be for those who are perishing, wine for those who are in anguish.*
>
> —PROVERBS 31:6

If they give you beer—then death is near:
And it's time to be heroic.
If they give you wine—You're totally fine:
You're just a whiny poet.

Linguistics

> *There are, it may be, so many kinds of voices in the world, and none of them is without signification.*
>
> —1 CORINTHIANS 14:10

The sounds of words . . .
The burst syllables
Heard like raindrops
In the crucible
Of the ear.
The pitter-patter
And the splatter of it.
The liquid vowels
And crackling consonants.
The vibrant verbs
In constant motion
And the adjectives
A laxative
For the constipated.
What a miracle language is!
Whether lyrical or posturing . . .
Profane or consecrated—
It alters on the altar
Of our offering.

Grief Is . . .

Give ear, O Lord, unto my prayer;
and attend to the voice of my supplications.

—PSALM 86:6

Molten magma bubbling beneath the crust.
An archaic alphabet of unsettled, unsettling dust.
A clarinet of sobs needing no translation.
The dumb phonetics of despair and desolation.
Some tongues proclaim prosaic platitudes
To comfort what remains uncomfortable.
For the suffering of those who suffer—
Is an attitude some find insufferable.

Yes, but Does He Write You Poetry?

> *There she lusted after her lovers, whose genitals were like those of donkeys.*
>
> —EZEKIEL 23:20

I thought I was endowed
With a decent, manly package.
But now I am quite cowed—
For I realize my lackage!
I told her it wasn't fair
And it felt a little wonky—
To judge me by the glare
Of a dude hung like a donkey.
Instead, I beg access me
For the quality of my verse.
You may measure all my *sonnets*:
Without a doubt, I'll come in first.

Cross-Stitch and Cross-Purposes

> *Then said Jesus unto his disciples,*
> *If any man will come after me,*
> *let him deny himself, and take up his cross,*
> *and follow me.*
>
> —MATTHEW 16:24

Your wife is a knitter—
And silently she counts her stitches.
But you, dear sir, had the misfortune
Of walking in on her
To ask an innocent question.
Standing chastised at the door,
You are quickly baptized
In a hiss of her hushes
And a string of chanted numbers:
"Twenty-two, twenty-three, twenty-four!"
She intones them at you in a voice
Thick with exasperation.
Her eyes are fixed on your form,
But you might as well be
An insignificant and lowly worm
Or beetle—as she glares at you,
Her stare piercing as a pointed needle.
Your wife, dear sir, is sitting on the sofa,
Covered in knitting material and cats.
It's like you've stumbled flat
Upon something mystically superior
And profaned it by your very existence!

Best to just slink back upstairs
Without any resistance
To your bread and circuses.
For your question will go unanswered
In the cross-stitched air—caught
In the snare of cross-purposes.

Red Stuff

And Esau said to Jacob, Feed me, I pray thee,
with that same red pottage; for I am faint

—GENESIS 25:30

Red snapper fish and red velvet cake—
The famous red apple; the slithering snake.
The blood in God's creatures—the sunset at dusk.
The Indian corn concealed in its husk.
The communist cadre—the red-headed girl.
The socialist padre—the Eurasian red squirrel.
The crimson tide and the precious red rubies.
The color of nipples—on some people's boobies.
The planet called Mars—the sports car for sale.
The fox in her den—your friend Abigail.
The stop sign on First St.—the pimple that popped.
Mao's little red book—the tomato you dropped.
The cherries and peppers—the grapes on the vine.
That sweater for Christmas with its horrid design.
The cat in the window—your heart and your kidneys.
And good old St. Nick—coming down the red chimney.

For What It's Worth

For we are saved by hope: but hope that is seen is not hope:
   —ROMANS 8:24

You flip the flashing coin—end over end—into the fountain.
Sun strikes copper as you make your wish—the penny
Hits the water and sinks to the bottom. It is autumn
And all things are returning to earth. For what it's worth
Your wishes have withered to a whimper. But when hope
Is a hard currency we remember a penny for our thoughts.
So many coins cast against gravity: terrestrial astronauts.

In Sickness and in Health

> *The spirit of a man will sustain his infirmity;*
> *but a wounded spirit who can bear?*
>
> —PROVERBS, 18:14

There are some things we simply can't sustain.
Endurance of the will is not always sustainable.
But what on earth can possibly have permanence?
And still, the heart continues to woo the brain
Despite all attempts to explain the unexplainable.
You are the center of my universe, contra Copernicus.
If I could take your suffering away, I would:
Bearing it in my flesh as a substitute:
Stigmata, Penance, Burnt Offering and Sacrifice.
So much in this life, wife, is poorly understood—
But love, though under duress, is never destitute.
Even in the face of hell it hopes for paradise.
Even in purgatory it yearns for heaven:
Even in this hospital, that burns like Armageddon.

Such Weariness

How much better to get wisdom than gold...

—PROVERBS 16:16

Sometimes, this world feels bent
And spent beyond repair—
Like a dirty coin too long
In circulation,
Mauled by money's mad and vicious
Songs of consumption.
Ambition is for the young—
But life *isn't* a ladder:
It's a seduction...
A romance of matter and spirit.
What we adore is what we become:
For God's sake, I can hardly bear it.

About the Author

Among other things, Daniel has been a community organizer and labor union activist, the lead singer/lyricist for the Indie rock band Mining for Rain, a poetry book reviewer for NewPages.com, and the poetry editor for *Sacramental Life* and *Doxology*.

His poems have appeared widely in journals and magazines, both online and in print, in Australia, the UK, and the U.S. He has a BA in Religion Studies with a minor in Theatre Arts from the College of Santa Fe in New Mexico and a Master of Divinity degree with a justice and peace studies concentration from the Iliff School of Theology in Denver. Daniel is also a professed religious brother in the Order of St. Luke, a dispersed ecumenical community rooted in the monastic tradition and dedicated to sacramental and liturgical education, scholarship, and practice.

He is the recipient of several literary honors, including two Purple Dragonfly Book Awards for Excellence in Children's Literature. In addition, out of approximately 150 entries, his poem "Lunch at Corafaye's" was one of only 11 poems chosen to be paired with a photographic interpretation by artist Sarah Jane Sanders and displayed on exhibit at the Norton Center for the Arts in Kentucky.

www.ingramcontent.com/pod-product-compliance
Lightning Source LLC
Chambersburg PA
CBHW071119090426
42736CB00012B/1958